HAVE YOU FIGURED IT OUT YET?

Do You Really Know Who and What You Are, Politically and Socially?

RICK LaRHETTE

ARCHWAY
PUBLISHING

Archway Publishing books may be ordered through booksellers or by contacting:

Archway Publishing
1663 Liberty Drive
Bloomington, IN 47403
www.archwaypublishing.com
1 (888) 242-5904

ISBN: 978-1-4808-7178-6 (sc)
ISBN: 978-1-4808-7177-9 (e)

Library of Congress Control Number: 2018913837

Print information available on the last page.

Archway Publishing rev. date: 12/07/2018

Contents

Introduction

After retiring, I took some time to reassess my life in general, including things like family, school, friends, marriage, career, and raising kids. One thought really piqued my curiosity: How did I develop as a person, politically and socially, and why? To do this, I asked myself dozens of questions and tried to answer them honestly and objectively. I decided to document my recollections, thoughts, and answers. As I watched the words fill my computer screen, I realized that it might be worthwhile to share these recollections, thoughts, and answers in the form of a book. I thought that some of the answers and the thinking behind them might have some value for my fellow Americans, but the real beneficiaries might be young adults who struggle with current political and social issues.

Reading today's news and social media reports is like drinking from a fire hose: much more flows than can be swallowed and digested all at once. Much of media goes well beyond informational, educational, and entertaining, delving into ideology, opinion, and hate speech with the specific intent of influencing a person's political and social thinking. No wonder people get confused and disgusted with politics and social media. Frankly, much of media now is a sewer.

I hope that you will learn as much by reading this book as I did by writing it. I now know exactly who I am, socially and politically. You may not agree with my thoughts and answers, but it might provide some fresh perspectives to consider. I tried to keep the book short, so a person can read it in two hours or less. It even contains some pictures and graphics.

Perhaps, reading about my quest may help you figure out who and what you are.

CHAPTER 1

Who Am I, Politically?

Political parties don't matter much; it all boils down to being liberal or conservative. How do you define *liberalism* and *conservatism*? Which one do I prefer, and why?

U ntil writing this book, I didn't have a clear idea where I was, politically or socially. Writing this book helped clarify things for me. Part of the problem was the many political and social choices that represent our personal ideology: Democrat, Republican, Independent, Libertarian, Socialist, Communist, etc. After thinking about this for a while, I realized the only important choices are whether to identify as liberal or conservative. In the past, each of the political parties had a mix of liberals and conservatives, but now that mix has almost disappeared. Now it is reasonable to say that most Democrats are Left-leaning liberals and most Republicans are Right-leaning conservatives. For that reason, I think our political parties should be renamed Liberal and Conservative, rather than Democrat and Republican.

Additionally, each party has its share of hardened ideologues, driving liberals further to the Left and conservatives further to the Right. The gap between liberals and conservatives has made talking more difficult and working together damn near impossible. Each side works to outmaneuver and demean the other side in a quest to gain favor with voters rather than working together to find the best solutions for the people. Just describing it makes me want to vomit! The widening gap between liberals and conservatives is driven by the extremes on both sides and amplified by their media supporters. After all, it makes for great news and gives the talking heads on both sides fodder for their well-paid biased opinions.

All that said, so let's begin. The first thing to do is define *liberalism* and *conservatism*.

There are literally hundreds of books and articles that have attempted to clearly define *liberalism,* so I had difficulty finding consistent definitions of the term. Where do you go to get a clear, unbiased definition? A dictionary, of course! That didn't go too well. I have several dictionaries collected over the years from my parents, my school years, and my work years. I started laughing out loud when I realized that dictionary definitions for *liberal* have morphed over the years. For example, the current definition of *liberal* (noun form) in a newer dictionary is "a broad-minded individual free from the restraints of dogma and tradition, open to new ideas, favoring proposals for reform, and tolerant of ideas and behaviors of others." An older dictionary states the definition as "a morally unrestrained and licentious individual." I've noticed lately that my liberal friends resent the negative connotation associated with the term *liberal* and now call themselves *progressive,* another nebulous term. Finally, the most recent definitions of *liberal* make such individuals sound like the most caring, intellectually superior, all-knowing, walk-on-water people on the planet. Then, I realized that people who write and revise our dictionaries and other information sources, such as textbooks, magazines, and newspapers, are overwhelmingly liberal intellectuals.

I found more consistent definitions of *conservatism* and the characteristics of conservatives in older and newer dictionaries. In general, *conservatism* is defined as "a philosophy that favors traditional values and institutions, is resistant to sudden changes, and is distrustful of government or judicial activism." Conservatives are often described as "cautious, restrained, less reactionary, and less emotionally driven." People and media critical of conservatives use descriptive words and phrases like uncaring, stubborn, uncompromising, stuck in the past, and opposed to change.

I was not satisfied with any of these definitions, so the only way to move forward with this book was to develop broader definitions of the terms *liberalism* and *conservatism,* in my own words and based on my own reading and research, life experiences, observations, and study of historical facts. The following are my personal definitions of both terms:

Liberalism is a system that emphasizes a strong federal government with social, political, and economic policies designed to solve people's problems. Liberal ideas are often driven by emotion and based on what I call *conceptual euphoria* (well-intended actions and programs that have not been thought out in advance). Liberals vigorously denounce social and economic inequality and believe that strong actions by the federal government, such as laws, programs, and regulations, are needed to control social inequalities and injustices. Liberal ideas are often thwarted by the US Constitution, and some liberals have taken up a position that the Constitution is antiquated and should be considered a "work in progress." Since modifications to the Constitution require ratification by at least three-fourths of the fifty states, liberals prefer to effect change through executive policy, regulation, and the appointment of justices with more-liberal interpretations of the Constitution. For example, some liberals want to get rid of the Second Amendment, which allows citizens the right to bear arms. Liberals know that getting three-fourths of the states to agree to this is impossible, so liberals promote a plethora of policies, laws, and regulations to make gun ownership as difficult as possible.

Conservatism is a system that emphasizes personal responsibility, limited federal government, and social, political, and economic policies that empower people to solve their own problems and pursue their own goals. Conservatives believe that the federal government's role is to provide a strong national defense, support traditional American values, ensure individual liberty, and promote the free-market economy. Conservatives demand that when laws, programs, and regulations are needed, they should be carefully crafted and cost effective. Conservatives believe in strict interpretation of the Constitution and its amendments, since we have worked to perfect them for 242 years.

Having attempted to define liberalism and conservatism in my own words, I now confess that I prefer conservatism, while not totally rejecting emotionally driven liberalism. This declaration did not come early in life; in fact, I didn't realize I was more of a conservative until my early thirties, when I started to pay more attention to news and politics.

Although there are positive attributes to both liberalism and conservatism, specific things really drove my preferred choice. For example, the War on Poverty started during the Lyndon Johnson (D) presidency in 1964. Johnson stated, "Our aim is not only to relieve the symptom of poverty, but to cure it and, above all, to prevent it." This so-called War on Poverty spawned ninety-two separate well-intended acts and government programs that resulted in a welfare state that has cost taxpayers approximately 15 trillion dollars, with only limited benefit. For example, the poverty rate (percentage of the population in poverty) has remained flat in a range of 10 to 15 percent from 1966 to 2015, according to government statistics. From an effectiveness standpoint, the War on Poverty has been a massive failure and has created long-term dependency on government welfare programs. Mounting criticism of the War on Poverty coming from conservatives finally led to the Personal Responsibility and Work Opportunity Act of 1996. President Bill Clinton (D) claimed this act "ended welfare as we know it."

Another recent example of unbridled liberalism without conservative thinking is the Affordable Care Act (Obamacare). It, too, had all the hopes of a well-intentioned liberal program, but without any conservative input, and now we know it was pitched to the American people under false pretenses to get it passed (you can keep your doctors and pay less). These examples contain all the earmarks of liberalism, such as well-meaning, emotionally driven conceptual euphoria, not fully thought out to anticipate unintended consequences, and lacking serious debate with conservatives before implementation.

While liberal and conservative ideas are necessary to make our government more responsive and effective, open dialogue and debate between liberals and conservatives is a predicate for successful outcomes. In other words, liberals and conservatives must talk and work together to find the best solutions for the American people.

> Continuing to vote for politicians with hardened un-compromising liberal or conservative ideology guarantees failure and the weakening of our republic.

CHAPTER 2

Walking My Talk

How did I apply my conservative values in life, career, and raising a family? Am I really a mix of liberal and conservative values? Did my conservative tendencies result in a more successful family outcome?

Okay, you know from the previous chapter that I prefer conservatism over liberalism. When my wife of forty-eight years and I had kids, we wanted them to grow up to be independent thinkers like us. We both instinctively knew that certain behaviors promote success in our American culture, regardless of a young person's developing philosophical and political preferences. We also knew that the family provides the first and, perhaps, the best programming for a young person's life.

My wife grew up in a traditional Irish-Catholic family in Boston. Her parents were politically active Democrats, and her father became president of a large union. Out of seven kids, she was next to the oldest and the only girl. Since her mother and father both worked, she became de facto mother, babysitter, coach, and defender for her younger five brothers at an early age. This experience helped make her tough, experienced, and streetwise before graduating from high school in 1966, two months after her seventeenth birthday. She discounted college because her family reserved educational resources for their sons. She went to work immediately after high school, starting with the telephone company and then moving to government service jobs in the Boston area, working for the navy, the draft board, and NASA's Electronic Research Center in Cambridge, Massachusetts. She believed in the value of hard work and did well in her government service jobs while living in her family home, contributing to the family, and continuing to care for her younger brothers. I met her on a blind date in 1968 while attending college in

Boston, and I married her in 1970. It wasn't too long after we met that I realized this was a special woman, someone to build a life and family with.

My family background was different from my wife's. I was adopted by my maternal grandmother shortly after my birth in 1947, in Bangor, Maine. Her daughter had given birth to me at an early age, so my grandmother and her second husband adopted me to provide a more stable and traditional family home. I always considered my grandmother and her husband to be my real mother and father, even after finding out I was adopted.

My parents had married shortly after my dad's return from his World War II service in the South Pacific. He had attended business school in Boston before the war, so he started a career working for General Foods Corporation as a sales representative after his return. My dad earned the reputation as an honest, ethical, and hardworking person during his thirty-seven-year career. My father's behavior during his career had a profound influence on my thinking and development as an adult.

Although our growing-up years were different, my wife and I brought some common values and thinking to our 1970 marriage, and I attribute this to the long-term success of our relationship. First, we both value family because, at the end of life, all you have left is family. Second, everyone makes friends during life, but who are your real friends? Well, both my wife and I have a handful of people we consider "real" friends. We each have hundreds of acquaintances, but real friends will show up at your wake/funeral even if they are inconvenienced. We don't think that religion or political ideology play an important role in choosing friends. However, people who filter their friends by extreme religious or political ideology are probably useful idiots of the extremes and should be avoided.

We have two daughters, born in 1971 and 1973. They grew up in a caring family that included loving grandparents and cousins galore. My wife and I exposed our girls to various environments in different locations as I pursued my career in the nuclear power industry. Initially, we didn't realize that exposing the kids to different environments would turn out to be a very good education.

Our first home in Maine was an older home that once was the telephone/telegraph office in a very rural area. We were surrounded by a turkey farm, a cattle/horse farm, and the Grange Hall. Our place was not a farm per se, but we did have a half-acre garden, a big apple tree, and a small barn where we raised free-range chickens and a beef animal the kids named Peekaboo. I was a member of the volunteer fire department and often drove the truck to fires because we lived near the firehouse.

Our second home was in Massachusetts, in a small community about forty miles outside Boston, near the Rhode Island border. We all remember this home well because of the winter of 1978, when we got fifty-two inches of snow in one storm. That blizzard locked us all in for a week. The storm gave us a chance to really get to know our neighbors and their kids. It was a continuous neighborhood block party, and the only way to get around was by snowmobile or snowshoes. Fortunately, we had a grocery store, drug store, and a bottle shop less than a mile away. The snow on the roads was so deep that it couldn't be plowed, and the town had to use bucket loaders and dump trucks to haul the snow away to clear the roads.

Our third house was in New Hampshire, where the girls got a top-quality elementary education, and we frequently went camping in the White Mountains with friends and their kids. We had a pool in the backyard and cookouts at least once a week, weather permitting. This drew family and friends to our place all the time. During this time, my wife enrolled in college, attended classes while the kids were in school, and graduated with honors.

Our fourth home was in Marietta, Georgia, where the girls each finished middle school and high school. We kept a boat on a nearby lake, and the kids enjoyed swimming, boating, waterskiing, and fishing. Sometimes my wife and I had dinner together on the boat during weekday evenings while the girls were at home studying (yeah, right!).

Our fifth home, where my wife and I still live, is in Acworth, Georgia, about thirty-five miles north of Atlanta. We built this as our retirement home, in 1998, a few years before I pulled the plug on working for someone else. When I retired at the end of 2006, at age sixty, I started a consulting business to bridge the time I until I turned sixty-five and would be eligible for Social Security and Medicare. At that time, I closed the business and became involved with classic cars, golf, fishing, traveling, cruising, and helping our kids raise their kids.

Fortunately, I had a career that allowed my wife to be a stay-at-home mom for most of my working years. My job required travel that took me away from home for one, two, or three weeks at a time. Even when I was at home, the job demanded some weekend work to meet schedules. Our kids observed firsthand what it took to be a husband-and-wife parenting team.

Both of our girls eventually married locally and still live close by. Each had two kids: one boy and one girl. We now have four grandchildren, ranging in age from nine to twenty-six. The whole family gets together frequently for family dinners, holidays, sporting events, and birthdays. Our oldest granddaughter recently gave us our first great-grandchild, a boy named Rhett. How good is that?

I share this personal information because it paints an important picture of how my wife and I walked our talk:

- Our successful forty-eight-year marriage has served an example for our kids, family, and friends.

- Our work ethic and personal values of honesty, faithfulness, responsibility, and accountability were modeled for our kids.
- Living in various locations and environments gave our kids a sample of all the possibilities: rural, suburban, and urban.
- Our typical responses to the demands of our kids when they were growing up included "No, you can't have that; if you want it, earn it"; "Only you are responsible for your actions"; "The choices you make now can affect the rest of your life"; and "You alone determine the quality of your future life."

The fundamentals of conservatism include personal responsibility, self-reliance, and a strong work ethic. We were not perfect parents, and we had our share of challenges. However, our two daughters are in their mid forties now, and they have good marriages, nice families, and good careers. My wife and I think that it is safe to say that our modeling of personal responsibility, self-reliance, and a strong work ethic have been adequately passed on. Additionally, our family motto, "A family that plays together stays together," has been realized. Despite the busy lives of our kids, we still get together for family dinners, birthdays, sporting events, and holidays.

For the most part, we have walked the conservative line in life, career, marriage, and raising a family. We taught our kids how to fish (be self-reliant). We taught our kids about the importance of family. We taught our kids what real marriage is all about. We taught our kids about the value of "real" friends.

If you are a senior, there is a good way to measure how you and your spouse measure up as responsible parents:

> If you did a good job raising your kids, you get to spoil your grandkids. If you did a poor job raising your kids, you may get the chance to raise your grandkids too!

CHAPTER 3

Choosing Your Political Party

Which party do I align with, and why?

S ome say we get our political party affiliation from our parents, and that is probably true early in life. Later, though, our political preferences evolve and may change. This is true for my wife and me.

My mother was an Episcopalian (the American version of the Church of England), and her family has a rich American history. Family members served in the Revolutionary War, the War of 1812, the Civil War, World War I, and World War II. She was a member of the Daughters of the American Revolution, and she was also an aspiring concert pianist until severe arthritis ended her career. Politically, my mother was a fiscal and social moderate who favored the Democrats. She hated Herbert Hoover (R) and loved and revered Franklin Roosevelt (D).

My father's family were Huguenots (French Protestants) who came to America in the mid-1800s and settled in the Boston area. Dad's grandfather was a medical doctor, and his father was in the import-export business. As mentioned, Dad was a World War II army veteran; he served in the South Pacific under MacArthur. After returning from the war, he met and married my mother, who was running a rooming house in Portland, Maine. My father had a strong work ethic and passed this trait on to me. Politically, my father was a fiscal and social conservative and a Republican. He encouraged me to give privately to a worthy cause of my choice, and to do so throughout my lifetime. After his death in 1980, I found out that he was a founding member of Boys Town and had contributed throughout his life.

Like my father, I picked a charity to support for a lifetime and have been quietly sponsoring dirt-poor kids and their families in Central and South America for many years, watching the kids go through elementary, middle, and high school. One has just entered college, which I find gratifying since sponsoring the child since the age of four.

As I've described, I met my wife on a blind date in 1968. I was then attending college in Boston, and she was the only girl in an Irish family with six brothers. Her father was president of the largest union in Boston, and they were Roman Catholics. Politically, they were Democrats and worked for and contributed to Democrat candidates in Massachusetts. However, they were what I call old-style democrats imbued with traditional conservative American values. I knew this when my wife's father confessed to me over a few drinks at a local Irish pub that he had secretly split his ballot and voted for Ronald Reagan, a Republican. As I was choking on my beer, he told me that he couldn't bring himself to vote for Jimmy Carter, a Democrat. Like my father, he served in the South Pacific during World War II, and his assigned navy ship sustained damage during a naval battle in the Philippines. He was not on board at the time because the navy required him to get circumcised before joining the ship in Philadelphia, where it received repairs from battle damage before heading back to the Pacific.

My wife's mother, my favorite mother-in-law, was a Democrat and voted a straight Democrat ticket in every national election. She was a wonderful person and a caring grandmother for our girls. We grew close over the years and had some interesting political discussions. She always voted for Democratic candidates and incumbents.

Initially, both my wife and I brought our political party affiliations to the marriage and often our votes canceled each other out: I was a Republican, and she was a Democrat. However, this didn't last long. As we matured and became more politically astute, we discussed the merits of people running in local, state, and national elections. More and more, our votes became more consistent, based on who was best regardless of party. Our criteria for choosing candidates became their personal positions on key issues, their values and character, and their promises and how well they followed through on them.

In 1980, when we lived in New Hampshire, I registered as a Democrat and voted against Ted Kennedy in the presidential primary. I couldn't bring myself to vote for a guy who, in 1969, let MaryJo Kopechne, a twenty-eight-year old teacher and campaign aid, die in a car Kennedy was driving after a drunken party on Martha's Vineyard. Kennedy was driving fast and went off the Chappaquiddick Island Bridge. He swam to safety and left MaryJo in the sunken car to suffocate.

When we moved to Georgia in 1984, we both supported and voted for Zell Miller, a Democrat, as lieutenant governor, governor, and, later, US senator. We admired him for his conservative values and his vigorous support of education, which resulted in the Hope Scholarship that pays tuition for students maintaining at least a B average in Georgia public colleges and universities. The Hope Scholarship is funded by the Georgia State Lottery. Additionally, we admired Zell Miller because he turned his life around, going from the drunk tank to the US Marine Corps. Later in life he said, "Everything you need to know I learned in the Marines." He later went on to earn degrees from the University of Georgia, and he taught history. Sadly, Zell Miller passed away in March 2018.

My wife and I no longer align ourselves with a specific political party. We are Independents and continue our practice of supporting and voting for the best people at the time, in local, state, and national elections, regardless of their party affiliation. We consider experience, accomplishments, character, adherence to the Constitution, ethics, and family values before we choose the person we will support.

CHAPTER 4

Choosing Your News and Information Sources

Where do I get my news and information from, and why? How much do news and information sources affect my views and positions over time? Can news and information sources be trusted?

I read and watch a wide variety of news and information sources, mostly online newspapers, cable news, and a few magazines. They range from the liberal (Left) to the conservative (Right). When newsworthy events occur nationally or internationally, I enjoy comparing how the Left and Right media present their factual news and opinions. Comparing Left and Right factual news is almost a hobby for me. The fun in this is not so much the factual news itself, for it is what it is, but the way it is presented—or "spun," as they say—is the interesting and entertaining part.

Let's define factual and spun news. *Factual news* is something that has happened or is happening; it is real and cannot be disputed. When media organizations don't like the factual news because it doesn't support their ideology or politics, they may choose to downplay it or not report it at all. *Spun news* is a form of propaganda designed to sway public opinion by providing a biased interpretation of the factual news, either positive or negative. To spin news, the media bring in like-minded experts to give their opinions; or, in the case of print media, invite their experts to write stories that are consistent with the media's political views.

Most news and information sources are biased to the Left or Right, so there is a danger of becoming unknowingly biased by relying on only one or two sources. Additionally, it is important to know where your chosen sources fall on the political scale. Sharyl Attkisson, an award-winning journalist and author known for her fearless reporting on untouchable subjects like media bias, put together a subjective chart in 2017, placing various media on a Far-Left to a Far-Right political scale. I found my information sources on her chart and eliminated the rest for simplicity. I also separated slight tilts Left or Right from Far-Right and Far-Left tilts. These are my current personal news and information sources, based on Attkisson's chart:

My Personal News and Information Sources, on a Political Scale

Liberal			Conservative	
Far Left	**Tilt Left**	**Middle**	**Tilt Right**	**Far Right**
MSNBC	AP	Roll Call	Barron's	Townhall
CNN	Reuters	Military Times	McClatchy	Newsmax
New York Times	Bloomberg	C-Span	Fox News	Breitbart
Washington Post	The Hill	UPI	The Federalist	OAN (One America News)
The New Yorker	Yahoo	Real Clear Politics	Washington Times	
Politico	CBS News	Wall Street Journal	The Daily Caller	
NBC News	ABC News		Forbes	
Slate	The Daily Beast		New York Post	
LA Times	People		Drudge report	
Huffington Post	ESPN			
Time				
NPR				

Based on chart found on www.SharylAttkisson.com

I was surprised and pleased that my news and information sources were distributed across the entire political spectrum, although most lean to the Left. Obviously, I don't spend all day viewing or reading these sources; rather, I refer to them on occasion. The two sources I consistently check each day are Yahoo News and Fox News: one that tilts to the Left and one that tilts to the Right, respectively. When there is big news, I check some of the others to become familiar with what the Left and Right are saying or not saying.

Understanding where your news and information sources fall on the political scale is essential if you want to be a well-informed American voter.

Conservatives have been railing for years that the media, in general, are liberal and lean to the Left, and there is a lot of evidence to support this. For example, Ken Stern, former CEO of National Public Radio (NPR) stated in an Associated Press (AP) opinion piece in late 2017 that "most reporters and editors are liberal." He went on to say that "a Pew Research Center poll found that liberals outnumber conservatives in the media by some 5 to 1, and that comports with my own anecdotal experience at National Public Radio (NPR)." (Note in the table above, NPR appears in the Far-Left column, based on Sharyl Attkisson's media bias analysis.) What impressed me most about Mr. Stern's media bias article was his brave venture into the land of conservatives (red zones), which makes up roughly 80 percent of the land area of the United States. For an entire year, he embedded himself with

NRA members and events, Tea Party members and meetings, evangelical church groups and activities, NASCAR events and folks, building homes for the homeless, and going wild pig hunting in Georgia. He said, "I found an America far different from the one depicted in the press and imagined by presidents ("cling to guns or religion") and presidential candidates ("basket of deplorables") alike." About his experiences with evangelicals, he said, "It left me with a very different impression of a community that was previously known to me only through Jerry Falwell and the movie *Footloose*." Regarding guns, he said, "Gun control and gun rights is one of our most divisive issues, and there are legitimate points on both sides. But media is obsessed with the gun control side and gives only scant, mostly negative, recognition to the gun-rights sides." The Far-Left media's hatred for the National Rifle Association (NRA), the symbol of gun owner rights and the Second Amendment, is well documented.

A recent Gallup poll found that only 40 percent of Americans trust the media to fairly and accurately report the news, and I believe that the media's overall tilt to the Left in news coverage and stories has a lot to do with that. I have struggled to understand this liberal bias for more than ten years, ever since my retirement. Having some free time to analyze this, I have developed an explanation using the Occam's Razor principle—among all the possibilities, the simplest explanation is probably the right one. Additionally, I dusted off my previous investigative skills by considering the who, what, where, when, how, and why aspects of the media's liberal bias.

Initially, it came down to simple geography. Many people have heard the term *coastal liberal,* and, for the most part, it is an accurate term for describing the liberal media. The main centers for both print and internet publishers are clustered in East Coast cities, from Boston to Washington DC, and on the West Coast, from Seattle down to San Diego. They are all deep blue (Democrat/Liberal) political areas that voted overwhelmingly for Clinton in the 2016 election. According to a *Politico* article, "The Media Bubble Is Worse Than You Think," published in May-June 2017, Clinton dominated where internet publishing jobs abound. Nearly 90 percent of all internet publishing employees work in a county where Clinton won, and 75 percent of them work in a county where Clinton won by thirty percentage points. When you add in the shrinking number of newspaper jobs, 72 percent of all internet publishing and newspaper employees work in a county that Clinton won. So, it doesn't take a genius to figure out why Clinton was the national media's candidate.

Okay, but geography alone cannot be the *root cause* of the media's liberal bias; so, I kept digging deeper and came up with the following:

- The first thing I investigated was the education of aspiring journalists. It is undisputed that liberal professors dominate academia, especially the liberal arts. A May 7, 2018 Fox News piece described a new study that found that 39 percent of top-tier liberal arts colleges in the United States don't have any Republicans on their faculties. The study conducted by the National Association of Scholars also found that the Democrat-to-Republican ratio was 10.4 to 1 among 8,688 PhD professors. The ratio is 12.7 to 1 when two military colleges, West Point and Annapolis, are removed from the sample. So, I concluded that students can easily become biased Left during the four to six years of their academic experience.

- Next, I thought about young journalism majors just beginning their careers. They all want to apply their skills and make a splash in their field. Many go where the big jobs are: the East and West Coasts. Regardless of their personal political or social leanings, they soon realize that stories need to pass muster with the bosses and be consistent with the biases of senior leadership and the norms of their media organizations. So, for these new journalists, it is either adapt or leave. Those who stay become what I call "institutionalized."

- Finally, I thought about how the people in Left-leaning media respond to their major mistakes and embarrassments. Clinton's unexpected loss in the 2016 election was a major embarrassment for the liberal media, and they have responded viciously. In concert with the Democrats and ever since the 2016 election, the liberal media have sought to undermine the duly elected president. I'm sure some efforts might have been made to look within and figure out the cause, but the internal biases were probably too strong to change. As a result, the liberal media might be embarrassed again this year (2018, as I write this) or in 2020. I don't think the liberal media, in general, have the courage to do what Ken Stern did (as described earlier in this chapter). They still have low regard for those outside the coastal liberal bubbles of wisdom in which they live. It has become evident that their liberal, superior, elitist, and condescending mind-set has made it impossible for them to really understand conservative America!

I think the root cause of liberal media bias is what I call "groupthink." Groupthink occurs when members of the group value harmony and coherence over accurate analysis and critical evaluation. Individual members of the group are strongly discouraged from any disagreement with the consensus; group members set aside their own thoughts and feelings to follow the word of the leader. Of course, groupthink can be found in all organizations, including Right-leaning news and information providers. However, there are many more Left-leaning news and information sources out there, resulting in an overall liberal bias in media.

I also don't think there is a short-term solution to the Left-leaning media bias. The absence of conservative professors in colleges and universities ensures a constant stream of liberal-minded young professionals in journalism, law, education, government, etc., for years to come.

I now need to share a few thoughts about the print media. I do read magazines, specifically *Time, People, Forbes,* and *The New Yorker.* I canceled my subscriptions to *Time* and *People* two years ago, but they still come in the mail every week or so. After reading some of the articles, I put them into the recycle bin. I used to read *Forbes* and *The New Yorker* on airplanes, but that source dried up when I retired; later, the airlines quit spending money on magazines anyway. Now, I read *Forbes* and *The New Yorker* in the waiting room of my doctor's office and in the "upscale" barbershop I frequent. *Time* and *The New Yorker* deserve some special comments. Over the years, *Time* has evolved into an extreme Left news and information source, and, for that reason, it is worth reading. *The New Yorker,* a Far-Left magazine, is a little too highbrow and elitist for me, but it gives me insight as to the mind-sets and thoughts of people in the liberal media bubble of New York.

Next, I want to share my thoughts on "fake news." The most egregious form of fake news is in the form of fabricated stories, which are often coupled with true facts to lend them plausibility and credibility. A famous example is the story about George W. Bush being away without official leave (AWOL) during his Air National Guard service. During Bush's run for reelection in 2004, Dan Rather—whose Left-leaning bias goes back decades—broke a story, based on forged documents, that claimed Bush was AWOL from his Texas Air National Guard duties back in 1973. The forged documents looked real but were created using a Microsoft computer font that didn't exist in 1973.

Refusing to admit the truth, Dan Rather lost his job as anchor of the *CBS Nightly News*. Another fake news example, far more significant and on a global scale, concerns what I will call "Climategate." Hackers released thousands of emails revealing that climate "scientists" were cooking the data and then worked with members of the media, especially the British Broadcasting Corporation (BBC), to sell their global warming theories. Our own Al Gore, former vice president of the United States, picked up the global warming banner, wrote a book scaring the hell out of people, and made millions selling this snake oil all over the world. The hacked emails showed that climate scientists greatly exaggerated the extent of human-caused global warming while privately admitting to one another that the evidence is nowhere near as strong as they would like. Since then, man-made climate change models have been found deficient, confirming that the great man-made global warming scare is not so much about science but political activism.

Groupthink and its characteristic consensus thinking played a role in both fake news examples described above.

The problem with fake news is that it is consumed by millions of people. Fake news is not limited to politics alone. The media provide a platform for stories about vaccinations and medications, stock market futures, weight loss, nutrition, etc. In recent years, fake news has been disseminated widely in late-night television, disguised as comedy. Think of the skits about President Trump or Sarah Palin: these are examples of fake news disguised as comedy on *Saturday Night Live*. It's hard to believe that some people take these skits as real news, but they do! And this trend continues.

Summing up, I can say I get my news and information from a wide variety of sources, most of them to the Left of center. I don't trust the media to provide objective news and information because most media are biased. I keep my conservative friends close and my liberal friends closer. Over the years, I have learned the dangers of relying on a single source for news and information. I suggest to my liberal family and friends that they should pay more attention to conservative media before making political judgments. Likewise, I recommend that my conservative family and friends do the same.

> Ask yourself, do you know and understand both sides before making conclusions and voting preferences?

CHAPTER 5

Choosing Your Friends

What barriers get in the way of friendships, and how do political and social views affect these relationships? Do your friends include people from all religious, political, and social belief systems?

You can't choose your family, but you can choose your friends. I consider myself fortunate to have many friends and to be blessed with a few very close friends. As I start my seventy-second trip around the sun, the meaning and value of friendship have become more and more important, even as some of the barriers to friendship have become more acute. In today's world, the internet, religion, and politics are major obstacles to friendship and the ability to have civil and thoughtful conversations.

Having many friends is a joy, but having a real friend is a gift. Let me share some personal thoughts on what I have learned over the years in regard to close friendships. A true friend is someone with whom you can discuss any subject in a nonjudgmental way. *Trust* is the key to real friendship. Trust means you can discuss issues that expose your own vulnerabilities or weaknesses without fear of betrayal or loss of confidentiality. You listen to each other and let each other finish a thought before speaking; no talking over each other. Critical traits like integrity, honesty, and empathy are givens between real friends.

I consider myself fortunate because I have four people whom I consider to be close "real" friends. Of course, one is my wife and soul mate of forty-eight years. One is a neighbor I have known for twenty years, whom I consider my brother from another mother. Another is a family member, one of my wife's brothers. The other person I have known for about sixty-five years; he was the best man at my wedding in 1970, in Boston. These are people I trust. I can talk about any subject with any of them, without holding back on anything and without being judged. Additionally, I am blessed to have another twenty or so people I consider good friends: some family and some former colleagues, and some others I see frequently to enjoy food, adult beverages, and classic car events.

Some people seem to struggle with social interaction because it is easier to stay connected with the world through their wireless devices. They view the internet as their real friend while avoiding direct social interactions that might lead to developing friendships. Adults may think that schools provide sufficient social interaction, but schools are very controlled environments that limit personal interactions to recess and lunch periods. Sports and other competitive activities are great, but, again, there is limited time for development of social skills, including development of real friendships. For young people who tend to be introverted, which may be half or more of all kids, the only real friend becomes a wireless device or a computer. In my younger days, we had the TV, and its use was generally during family time when there was some human interaction. An exception was Saturday morning cartoons. After finishing homework, I could go outside to play with neighborhood kids until the streetlights came on. There were significant social interactions during this time, including some good friendships, arguments, and a few fights.

Religion has been, and still is, a major divider in terms of friendships and social interactions. In some countries, religious beliefs provide an excuse for hate and war. We have all heard divisive religious proclamations like the following:

- My God is the only true God, and my religion is the only true religion.
- It is your duty to kill Christians and Jews if they refuse to convert.
- Catholicism is the only true Christian religion.
- Hard to believe Christians believe a dead Jew rose from the dead.
- You shouldn't associate with or marry outside your religion.

All I can say about this can be summed up as follows: If your religion requires you to shun or hate someone, you need to get a new religion!

I, for one, have not rejected my Christian faith, only my church. The same is true for my wife. We both have faith in Jesus Christ and model our lives as best we can to live His ministry of peace and love. I have evolved to a point where I no longer need a church and a priest, minister, or rabbi to guide and confirm my faith. Besides, we all have seen the sick and depraved actions of religious leaders who commit pedophilia, or preach violence in the name of God. However, I have no problem or complaints with folks who attend church regularly because it is a social meeting place of like-minded people who seek friendship and human interaction, which most of us crave.

I believe politics and a raft of ideological issues have become the new "religion" for many who have walked away from their religious beliefs. As a result, politics has become a new powerful barrier to civil discourse and friendships. I have many friends of all religious and political persuasions. For about the past forty years or so, religion has not been a significant factor in relationships and open dialogue among my friends. I can't say the same for politics. For example, when I retired twelve years ago, a few of my former colleagues began having breakfast together once a week. This practice continues today, and the number of participants has increased over the years. In addition, we started doing monthly lunches with turnouts ranging from twenty to thirty-five people. Occasionally, religion would come up in conversations but never resulted in heated discourse or shut down subsequent dialogue. However, when someone had the courage to bring up politics, I recall a few times when liberal and conservative group members started to go at it verbally. Fortunately, it never turned ugly. But, remember, these people worked with each other for years. From this, I concluded that the riskiest subject for conversation at social events is politics, not religion.

Self-righteousness has no place in any friendship, so I recommend politely walking away if you meet this type of person. We see people like this all the time in print, on the internet, on cable news, in religion, in schools, in colleges and universities, in politics, and at the mall. I can honestly say that people like this whom I have met or have known are typically, but not always, liberals who see themselves as superior, more broad-minded, better educated, and more caring than others.

In my experience, there is nothing worse than people who only see the bad or less-than-perfect side of things. No one enjoys a humorless, pessimistic, cynical, bitter person because it becomes nearly impossible to have an open conversation with someone like that. When you try to engage with such individuals, they drag you down emotionally. They are driven by hate and refuse to listen to other opinions or facts that don't support their beliefs. Yes, I am talking about liberals and their subgroups (Democrats, Socialists, Communists, Marxists, some liberal Republicans, the mentally disturbed, and most of the media). Anyone who watches the news or trolls the internet for news and information cannot deny this. It's out there for all to see every day. Most of it consists of hate the president, hate the vice president, hate conservatives, hate Republicans, hate the president's family, hate the president's communications director, hate the senate majority leader, hate the Speaker of the House, and hate those who practice religion. The media spin most favorable news into something negative, or just ignore it; and they generate fake news for impact before retracting the lies when they get caught.

For my younger fellow Americans out there, I recommend developing friendships with people of all religious and political beliefs. You will benefit from diverse opinions and views. However, please don't delve into deep religious or political discussions until the friendship matures or the discussion is mutually desired. Learn to politely back away from the self-righteous or strongly opinionated because real friendship will not be possible unless some of your views and opinions align.

I cannot stress the importance of real friendship. Although you may think you have many friends, you need a real friend or two to have open and trusting discussions on any topic, including politics, religion, or deeply personal issues. Being open with a real friend is good for your well-being, including your mental health. It's much better than paying thousands of dollars to psychiatrists or other professionals to do what a trusted friend or soul mate can probably do for free. Finally, please don't diminish the value of a real friend because they are rare! Besides, real friends will show up at your funeral and may even volunteer to coordinate final arrangements for your spouse or kids.

Friendship is not something you learn in school. If you haven't figured out the real meaning of friendship, you still have a lot to learn.

Choose your friends wisely and nurture those true close friends! Walk away from the self-righteous and those who cannot tolerate other views and opinions.

CHAPTER 6

The Role of Federal Government

What are my thoughts on the role of our federal government? What is the best type of government for our American culture (socialism, capitalism, or communism)?

I will approach these questions with some historical perspective. In simple terms, the role of the federal government in the United States is defined by our Constitution as a sharing arrangement between a centralized federal government and the individual states. In the Constitution, certain powers are delegated to the federal government because they apply to all citizens and states. These powers and prerogatives include the following:

- Protection of citizen rights and privileges, and abolishment of slavery
- National defense, foreign relations, and commerce, treaties, and prosecution of war
- Establishment of a federal court system and a supreme court to resolve disputes
- Establishment of a universal monetary system
- Copyright protection
- Creation of a postal system with roads to deliver
- Establishment of a common system of weights and measures
- Taxation to raise revenue to carry out federal functions

The Tenth Amendment to the Constitution limits the federal government to the specific functions and prerogatives listed above. Remaining functions are reserved for the states and individual citizens.

In determining the best type of government for our culture, you must understand that the United States was founded as a republic, not a pure democracy. If you recite the Pledge of Allegiance, you will recognize this.

The definition of *democracy* is "a state in which all major decisions are made by majority vote of all citizens." In a true democracy, the majority rules in all cases, regardless of any consequences for individuals or for those who are not in the majority on an issue. Some say that pure democracy is "mob rule," and mob decisions may or may not be best for the country and its citizens. The Founding Fathers recognized this and designed our government to be a *representative republic* based on principles of a democracy. The definition of *republic* is "a representative form of government that is ruled according to a constitution."

There is a profound difference between a republic and a pure democracy, as seen above. For this reason, the Founding Fathers divided power between a House of Representatives made up of elected members from each state (number based on population), a Senate with two members elected from each state to provide advice and consent, an executive (president and vice president) elected by the people to lead the republic, and a judiciary to ensure that acts, policies, and regulations passed by the House, Senate, and executive branch are consistent with our Constitution.

Anyone trying to determine what form of government is best for us must first define the alternatives, such as socialism, capitalism, or communism, and then determine if that form of government is compatible with our culture and Constitution.

My definitions for the basic forms of government are as follows:

SOCIALISM

Socialism is a concept where individuals don't have ownership of land, capital (money), or industry. Instead, the whole community collectively owns and controls all property, goods, and means of production. In theory, all share equally in work and the fruits of their work. Ideally, socialism is consistent with Judeo-Christian values of sharing equally and helping the poor and needy, while eliminating greed, competition, and jealousy. However, this concept ignores powerful forces like freedom that make up the human spirit.

One example in our history vividly points out the major shortfall of socialism. The Plymouth Colony was established by the Pilgrims in 1620. The writings of the first governor of the Plymouth Colony, William Bradford, describe how the people initially decided to start a community garden and share the vegetables and fruit equally at the end of the growing season. Many of the colonists were not interested in plowing, planting, and weeding because the garden was not theirs. As a result, the garden was not well tended, and the crop yield was far less than expected. By 1623, the colony was facing starvation and decided to take a new approach. Each family was allotted a piece of land proportioned according to family size, and they would be allowed to keep their crops for themselves and barter any excess. Family members, including children, willingly worked in their gardens, and crop production improved greatly. The lesson learned, as described by William Bradford, was that if you own it, you take pride in it and take care of it. The Pilgrims started out with socialism for the first two years but abandoned it in favor of what we now call capitalism.

CAPITALISM

Capitalism is an economic system where individuals, small business, and corporations can own and control land, capital (money), production, and distribution of goods. Operational costs are funded by profits, which are held in check by competition between others that provide similar goods or services. In a capitalistic system, people have the freedom to do what they want, live where they want, and have what they want. People are free to pursue their dreams without government interference, and people have maximum choices in life. This is the "pursuit of happiness" granted in the Declaration of Independence.

A recent example of this is Apple, which started as Apple Computer Company. Two young men, Steve Jobs and Steve Wozniak, had the idea that people would like to have their own personal computers at a reasonable cost. They got startup funding ($250,000.00) from a wealthy capitalist (Mike Markkula) and built their prototype computer in a garage. Sales took off immediately after production started. By September 2011, Apple was employing forty-eight thousand people, had annual sales of more than 65 billion dollars, and became the largest publicly traded company in the world and the largest technology company in the world, measured by revenue and profit. Capitalism allowed these folks to raise funds, build a prototype computer, and develop means for production and distribution. They created wealth for themselves, their employees, and their stockholders without stealing money from anyone. They became rich by following their dream, creating a new product, creating a new company, creating new jobs, and creating new wealth for thousands of employees and millions of investors.

CAPITALISM turns luxuries into necessities.

SOCIALISM turns necessities into luxuries.

COMMUNISM

Communism is a more extreme version of socialism. Like socialism, individuals in a communist system cannot own land, capital, or industry. Under communism, the government has total control of everything, including what is produced, and who will receive the goods and services. The communist government decides where you live and what you do. Individuals have few if any rights. Therefore, any further discussion of communism is not necessary because it is incompatible with American culture, our Constitution, and the Bill of Rights (the first ten amendments to the Constitution).

Before moving on, let me share some direct observations of communism from several technical-assist visits to then Eastern Bloc countries (the Soviet Union and others) in support of a US Department of Energy contract to improve safety at Russian-designed nuclear power plants. The friends I made during my visits to Russia, Ukraine, and Bulgaria in the mid-1990s revealed to me how much these people envy the freedoms and access to goods we enjoy in the West. One vivid example is permanently imprinted in my mind. My team was visiting a Russian nuclear power plant hundreds of miles southeast of Moscow. It was wintertime. The first thing we noticed was that dozens of cars in the plant parking lot had frozen to the ground in several inches of ice. The next thing we noticed were shoddy government-built high-rise apartment buildings for plant employees. The final thing noticed was a government-owned general store with sparsely filled shelves. As we got to know our Russian counterparts, they told us that the government had provided them with a free college education, sent them to the plant as operators, assigned them an apartment in the living complex next to the plant, and provided a subsistence living. Many had not received a paycheck in recent months, so the government was currently providing cars and refrigerators as compensation. They told us that gas was expensive or unavailable, so their cars were not used much; most things they had were bought or bartered on the black market, and access to the internet was severely limited and tightly controlled.

Thereafter, I hosted a visit for these same people to come to the United States to tour a nuclear power plant. I was shocked, but not too surprised, by their reaction during a visit to a Super Walmart near Lawrence, Kansas. They stated they had never seen a store so fully stocked with groceries, electronics, hardware, clothing, over-the-counter drugs, adult beverages, and gardening and yard supplies. Most of them bought items to take back to their families and took copious photos of the abundance to show family and friends back home.

I believe the best form of government for American culture is capitalism with appropriate restraints on human excesses, particularly greed and avarice. Socialism and communism diminish the human spirit, the will to work, competition, innovation, and creativity, so they are inconsistent with American values.

If you recall, I previously discussed the War on Poverty (in chapter 1) and said that it spawned ninety-two congressional acts and programs that led to the so-called welfare state. In my mind, one of these, Medicare, meets the intent of the Constitution because it "promotes the general welfare" of all *retired* citizens in all states. Similarly, Social Security, which was passed well before the War on Poverty began, also "promotes the general welfare" of all *retired* citizens in all states. Both programs were born, in part, from socialist thinking but meet the constitutional criteria for the role of the federal government, even though they were not specifically called out in the Constitution or the supporting documents (Federalist Papers). Additionally, these programs are paid for by people during their working lives through payroll deduction. The government's role is just to hold funds for people until they retire.

Government's most important duty is to protect the people, not control their lives.

CHAPTER 7

Immigration

What are my views on immigration, and why?
Should our borders be controlled, and how?
What type of people should we invite into the
United States?

Today, our immigration system is broken, and everybody knows it. Individuals and families who enter our country the right way and play by the rules watch others illegally bypass the rules. Business owners who offer their workers good wages and benefits see the competition exploit undocumented immigrants by paying them far less. Undocumented (illegal) immigrants who desperately want to embrace the American dream remain in the shadows, or risk their families being torn apart.

The widely held belief that immigration and immigration reform are so complex that they defy a political solution is a load of crap. Let me reduce this issue down to a few pages.

I am a fan and promoter of legal immigration. We are a country of roughly 330 million people, based on 2017 government population data. We have the largest economy in the world, and we need inflow of new people to supplement the existing birthrate. Currently, we see record low unemployment and record employment because of current political and economic policies. This tells anyone with a modicum of common sense that we need to import employable talent to supplement our workforce. This means our immigration system must invite skilled and educated people into the United States to keep our economy growing and moving forward. What we don't need are millions of uneducated and unskilled people who need taxpayer assistance to live. We know from experience that it may take one to three generations for these people to adapt, get educated/trained, and assimilate into our culture. We also know that many of these people will be unsuccessful, and they may resort to crime and violence to exist within our borders.

The United States has a process for foreigners to apply for legal immigration and eventual citizenship. Those who choose to ignore our legal immigration rules and bypass our immigration laws do not deserve special treatment and should be immediately deported. The United States is a sovereign country, and we have the right to establish the rules for legal immigration and protect our borders against illegal immigration.

There are many reasons that we have not been able to resolve the issue of illegal immigration. Here are a few:

- **Congressional failure** to fund effective barriers that prevent illegal border crossings
- **Liberals/Democrats and some Republicans** who accept the concept of open borders and globalism
- **Democrats** looking for votes by providing benefits for illegals and protection in sanctuary cities
- **Greed** of farmers and others looking for cheap labor and higher profits without consideration for longer-term consequences for our country
- **People** hiring illegals, knowing that their green cards, Social Security numbers, and other credentials are probably fake

- **Chambers of commerce** and other similar pro-business groups that support use of cheap labor regardless of consequences
- **Lobbyists** influencing and corrupting politicians to promote globalism and open borders
- **Local, state, and federal politicians** willing to be corrupted and bribed by campaign contributions, gifts, and favors

The above reasons, and many others, for not solving the immigration problem provide a formidable force that defies common sense. Most Americans and all people I know want a permanent solution to illegal immigration and a reasonable process for legal immigration. It seems to me that when the majority of the electorate wants a solution, but the political class can't deliver, there is something rotten going on. My favorite Democrat president, Harry Truman, found that the root cause of seemingly unsolvable political issues, like immigration or health care, is simple greed. Politicians get corrupted by generous campaign contributions that get funneled into foundations and other financial entities controlled by the politician.

> # There is no legal way to get rich in politics unless you're a criminal.

To break the immigration logjam, we need a strong, uncorrupted executive leader like President Trump to apply continuous pressure on Congress for a fix. The president has provided an outline of an immigration bill that he will sign, but Congress has been unable to get enough votes to get it passed. The president is right: more reasonable uncorrupted Republicans must be elected to break the logjam. Democrats and some liberal Republicans will not vote for any immigration bill supported by the president because they support open borders and cheap labor, and they appreciate generous campaign contributions, gifts, and favors.

The federal immigration system determines the people who enter the country, and how many of them can enter. It also decides who can apply for permanent visas for family and relatives. Immigration policy must be a federal responsibility. Delegating immigration policy and laws to individual states would result in chaos; think about California.

Okay, here is my dose of common sense to help resolve the immigration debacle:

- Immediately fund and build the wall along the Mexican border. Maximize the use of technology and hire more border agents, as needed.
- Effective immediately, people from any other country who enter the United States illegally will *never* be granted amnesty, legal status, or a path to citizenship. This should help stem the flow of new illegals while the wall is being built.

- Eliminate sanctuary cities and arrest and prosecute state, city and town officials who refuse to cooperate with ICE and other federal government officials.
- Illegals in the United States who have been previously deported should be apprehended, imprisoned, and/or permanently deported without any hope of ever becoming legal immigrants.
- Illegals without valid green cards (legal status) currently living in the United States must register as such within thirty days or be subject to arrest and immediate permanent deportation.
- Illegals who have resided in the US for two or more years and have no criminal record must apply for legal status within thirty days or be permanently deported.
- Eliminate current "chain migration" and the immigration "lottery" programs.
- Adequately staff US embassies to process applications for legal immigration and asylum requests.
- Implement merit-based immigration standards. Immigrants with skills and education useful to the United States should be given priority for legal immigration and eventual citizenship.

CHAPTER 8

Education

Do young people have sufficient knowledge of our government to make informed voting decisions? What are my thoughts on the purpose of education—liberal arts vs. technical/engineering, college degrees vs. technical/vocational training and/or apprenticeships? What changes, if any, should be made to primary, secondary, and college curricula?

T he purpose of American education is to provide people with the knowledge and skills needed to succeed in our culture and become good citizens. In my view, the most important part of our early educational process should consist of reading, writing, arithmetic, and civics. Yes, *civics,* the study of the rights and duties of citizens and of how government works. Civics should be introduced and expanded incrementally in the curricula of grades 1 through 12. By the time a person graduates from high school, he or she is old enough to vote (or probably will be by the subsequent Election Day) and should be able to easily pass the test given to immigrants as the last required step for US citizenship.

I recommend that you take the citizenship test as a way of evaluating the quality of your own civics education. You can take the test online by going to USCitizenshipSupport. com. The website offers a hundred-question test, with answers, and a ten-question quiz randomly selected from the citizenship-question database. The database of questions covers the following topics related to the United State: government, history, geography, symbols, and national holidays. If you do poorly on the test, your primary and secondary education failed you in regard to an important part of an American education.

Frankly, our educational system has been degraded by overly focusing on the development of knowledge and deemphasizing the importance of developing skills. American parents pushed their kids toward college and a four-year degree, in an attempt to ensure a better life, while discouraging technical/vocational education that is focused on employable skills. Working with your hands was universally seen as something related to lower-class occupations. The stigma of working with your hands continues today. Parents saw college degrees as much more prestigious and promising for their kids, especially when earned from Ivy League or major universities. When kids want this for themselves, it's fine. The only problem I have with this is when it directs kids onto educational paths they are not suited for or don't really want. This seems to be the case more often than not, since about half of kids who enter colleges and universities these days do not graduate. To be honest, leaving college after a year or two is no better than having a high school diploma with respect to employment.

Some students who graduate from college obtain worthless liberal arts degrees. They have no employable skills or job prospects when they finish college, even though they have college degrees. These students are then forced to obtain graduate degrees with better prospects for employment and better compensation, or they just live in their parents' basements until they figure out what they really want to do in life. I am not against liberal arts courses and degrees, just the false expectation that a liberal arts degree alone prepares a person to enter the workforce with skills that employers want and need.

The tragedy is that kids who pursue worthless degrees or drop out of college accumulate huge student loan debt. Our government currently backs more than 1.5 trillion dollars in student loan debt. Since roughly half of students who enter college do not graduate, a significant portion of this debt owned by taxpayers goes to waste. Some of this debt may never be repaid, leaving taxpayers with the bill.

I think colleges and universities have been irresponsible with respect to costs. The academic elites who run colleges and universities have been able to raise tuition and other education fees because politicians have created government programs that allow students to borrow huge amounts of money to get an education. As a result, tuitions have increased about five hundred times the rate of inflation since I went to school. For example, currently, a liberal arts degree (BA) typically costs about eighty thousand dollars at a major university, and I have already discussed the practical value of a liberal arts BA degree without additional graduate studies and degrees. In addition, colleges and universities have spent millions—billions nationally—on new facilities and elaborate campuses to attract new students and faculty.

I also believe that colleges and universities have become warehouses for liberal elitists who work with their brains instead of their hands. It is hard to assess the educational impact of this situation except to say that I have seen interviews with students who say that they have learned to provide answers and responses to their liberal professors to get the grades without revealing their own personal and more conservative beliefs. As I've already shown, the facts confirm the dominance of liberal thinking in colleges and universities. For example, a study by the National Association of Scholars found that the Democrat-to-Republican (D:R) ratio was 10.4 to 1 among 8,688 PhD professors. The ratio is 12.7 to 1 when two military colleges, West Point and Annapolis, are removed from the sample. The highest D:R ratio of all is for the most ideological field: interdisciplinary studies. "There was not a single Republican in fields like gender studies, black studies, and peace studies," declared the National Association of Scholars' study. Additionally, a recent survey found that 39 percent of top-tier liberal arts colleges don't have a single Republican/Conservative professor on the staff. I don't get hung up on statistics, but they do provide a valid indicator of the ideological/political makeup of academia. This situation gives me concern because college and university cultures are so biased toward liberalism and academic elitism.

> Colleges and universities are supposed to be centers for learning, not political and social indoctrination centers.

I feel qualified to discuss this issue because I have a vocational/technical education *and* a university education, obtained during the period from the late 1960s to the early 1980s. I like to work with my hands *and* my brain. Advice given to me by guidance counselors in high school was worthless;

basically, these educational elites preached against working with your hands if you were a student with college potential. Frustrated, I took total control of and responsibility for my own future educational endeavors and pursued a technical career in electrical and nuclear technology. Educational costs were reasonable back then, and I was able to pay off my student loans in less than five years. I was also very fortunate to work for a nuclear power plant owner who wanted to raise the education level of the plant's nuclear reactor operators from a two-year degree (associate's degree) level to a four-year (bachelor's degree) level, at no cost to the employees.

> I want to remind you that a university is not the only place where you can enrich your mind or prepare yourself for the real world. It's merely the *most expensive* place.

The biggest obstacle for any young person to overcome is the parents' vision of a six pack–toting, knuckle-dragging laborer in dirty coveralls. Parents want something better than that for their kids. There is a critical need for skilled labor, especially those skills that require valuable credentials, such as master electrician, master plumber, master technician, certified computer technician, licensed nuclear reactor operator, certified HVAC technician, licensed dental hygienist or assistant, and dozens more. These are technical professionals who make our lives better and go home after work knowing that they produced or created something worthwhile, fixed something that wasn't working, and provided a valuable service to fellow citizens. It is a serious mistake to assume that skilled, credentialed technical people don't make a good living. In fact, I can attest that skilled professionals without a bachelor's degree can and do make a very respectable living. Additionally, technical professionals usually leave work behind at the end of the day, unlike many college-educated professionals who take work home and work many uncompensated hours because it is built into their salaries.

It is unfortunate that colleges and universities have been slow to adopt the merits of working with the hands instead of the brains. As a result, America has seen the emergence of independent vocational-technical schools focusing on skill development, and technical colleges that combine mind and skill development in their curricula. I highly recommend this type of postsecondary education for students who reject the idea of getting their minds pumped full of mush, going into debt, and graduating without marketable skills.

I also admire and have great respect for companies and unions that have started apprenticeship programs in the skilled trades, including electrical, plumbing, construction, welding, and many others. While these programs may not include liberal arts courses, they do a good job of providing technical knowledge and skills while getting on-the-job experience at the same time.

Whatever you decide to do in life, be the best you can!

In my view, there is no excuse for any person not to get some type of skill/education beyond high school that provides a good living and a future. There is no reason why a person can't start with a skill and seek further education over time to advance the career if desired.

Rick LaRhette

CHAPTER 9

Environmentalism/ Global Warming

What are my views on environmentalism and global warming? Has global warming been exaggerated? How have politics and the media affected these issues?

I am a lifelong environmentalist, at least since graduating from high school in 1965. Every American wants and deserves clean water and clean air. I remember when the Penobscot River that flows through my hometown of Bangor, Maine, was so polluted in the 1960s that the salmon gave up coming upstream to spawn. The river was also a source of drinking water. I also remember when the Cuyahoga River in Ohio caught fire in 1969 because of oil slicks. This river had a history of catching fire, going back to the 1950s. Americans finally realized that the federal government needed to step in to establish nationwide pollution standards for waterways. As I recall, the independent Environmental Protection Agency (EPA) was created in late 1970 by Republican President Richard Nixon, by executive order. This prompted bipartisan support in Congress and resulted in strong environmental laws that resulted in and amazing cleanup of rivers and streams. Subsequently, the EPA developed clean-air standards that resulted in much cleaner and safer air to breathe. I am proud to say this is a great example of bipartisan executive and congressional action that improved our environment. I am a happy guy now because the salmon have returned to the Penobscot River and there are no more fires on the Cuyahoga River.

During the last forty or so years, the success of the EPA has inspired many people to become environmentally minded. I am one of those people, and that is one of the reasons I chose my career in nuclear energy. Nuclear power plants do not pollute our water or our air. Producing power by nuclear fission replaces the need to burn coal, natural gas, and oil to produce electricity, run our vehicles, heat our homes, and run our industries. Nuclear power plants do not produce carbon dioxide (CO_2) and other greenhouse gases, which are by-products of burning coal, natural gas, and oil. Unfortunately, many people fear and object to nuclear power, and they have been effective emotionally and politically in limiting its use and expansion. Political pressure from antinuclear activists over the years has resulted in increased costs because of legal challenges and burdensome regulations, making the cost of building a new nuclear power plant noncompetitive with burning fossil fuels like coal and natural gas. Limiting nuclear power development is forcing electric utilities to continue to build new cleaner coal and natural gas units while retiring older dirtier generators. What is forgotten or hidden is the fact that new fossil-fueled units do a good job reducing particulate pollution but do not eliminate it. They continue to produce greenhouse gases, just like the older units. If you live in or near a big city like I do, you can still see the yellowish-brown haze near sunset on a hot summer day with no wind. These are particulates in the air we breathe!

Before moving on, it is important to understand which specific greenhouse gases we eject into the atmosphere. Whenever we burn fossil fuels like natural gas and oil to heat our homes, produce electricity, run our cars, and power airplanes, we produce what are called *man-made greenhouse gases*. These consist of CO_2, nitrous oxides, and a few others in smaller quantities. These gases, especially CO_2, combine with air (20 percent oxygen, 80 percent nitrogen, and water vapor). CO_2 contributes to our atmosphere's ability to allow solar energy in while limiting its ability to escape back into space.

What many people don't know, or don't appreciate, is that water vapor, also known as humidity and clouds, is the most important and powerful greenhouse gas, dwarfing the effects of man-made greenhouse gases. Without huge amounts of water vapor in our atmosphere, the earth would be barely habitable, with extremely dry days and extremely cold nights.

The thought that CO_2 is a gas that can help trap heat in our atmosphere provided a wealth of possibilities for opportunists to speculate that CO_2 produced by man will doom the earth to increasing temperatures, converting livable areas to desert, melting the polar ice caps, flooding low-lying coastal cities, reducing the number of farmable areas, and eventually leading to the extinction of humans. A classic example is a former vice president of the United States, Al Gore, who wrote the book *An Inconvenient Truth.* I mentioned Gore earlier, but let's look at this further now. Gore made millions from the book and well-paid presentations all over the world. University researchers saw an opportunity to get grants to study this, which is a good thing. We saw the emergence of the term *global warming* after the media got a hold of the issue, resulting in story after story about our impending doom. Subsequently, more and more evidence emerged that the original scientific proclamations about global warming were based on the consensus of climate scientists rather than actual scientific evidence. Further scientific study and research revealed that global average temperatures were not increasing as originally predicted, and that the computer models used to predict future warming were seriously flawed. This entire episode provides a classic example of what happens when politics and media run with false assumptions.

Recently, some sanity has returned to global weather science and predictions. The ridiculous thought that *all* warming was man-made, and that we were on the verge of doom, was finally rejected based on real science, not opinions and consensus. Actual data confirms that average global temperatures have barely risen over the past fifty years, less than one degree Celsius, according to the best estimates by National Aeronautics and Space Administration (NASA) and National Oceanic Atmospheric Administration (NOAA).

Reliably measuring global average temperature rise is not only complex but almost impossible if you use some common sense and some known facts. First, the land area of the planet is only 29.2 percent, meaning 70.8 percent of the earth is covered by ocean. Second, man-made greenhouse gases that contribute to global warming are mostly centered in eastern Asia, Europe, and the US, which, together only account for a small portion of the total planetary land area. Additionally, greenhouse gases are not spread uniformly throughout the entire planetary atmosphere instantly; this mixing takes a lot of time, perhaps months or years. The fundamental truth here is that localized man-made greenhouse gas emissions can affect the local environment—case in point, Beijing and Los Angeles, for example. The effects globally are much less significant. As a result, I don't place too much credibility on global average temperature calculations, but I accept them as best estimates.

Let's now take a *factual* look at the sources of man-made greenhouse gases from the EPA:

Total US Greenhouse Gas Emissions by Economic Sector in 2016

Source of Greenhouse Gas Emissions	Portion
Transportation Fuels (Cars, Aircraft, Trucks, Trains)	28%
Power Plant Fuels (Coal, Natural Gas, Oil)	28%
Industrial Fuels (Coal, Natural Gas, Oil)	22%
Residential/Commercial Heating Fuels (Oil, Natural Gas)	11%
Agriculture	9%
Other	2%

Referring to the above chart, you can see that 72 percent of greenhouse gas emissions in the US are produced by automobiles, airplanes, trucks, industrial facilities, home and commercial building heating systems, and farming activities (methane from farm animals). Surprisingly, total greenhouse gas emissions from US power plants only represent 28 percent of the total. Nevertheless, it is worth looking more closely at electrical power production because power plants seem to get the worst reputation with respect to man-made greenhouse gas emissions.

The US Energy Information Agency provided a breakdown of electrical power production for calendar year 2017. About 63 percent of this electricity generation was from fossil fuels (coal, natural gas, petroleum, and other gases). About 20 percent was from nuclear energy, and about 17 percent was from renewable energy sources.

The only sources of electrical power generation that do not contribute to water and air pollution and greenhouse gas generation are nuclear, hydro, wind, solar, geothermal, and photovoltaics (convert the sun's energy directly to electricity). Some of the renewable power sources like biomass, landfill gas, wood, and solid waste produce about 1.7 percent of our electrical energy but also contribute to pollution and greenhouse gas emissions.

As an environmentally minded person, I know that man-made greenhouse gases do contribute to global warming, albeit a relatively small amount. I know that the largest source of CO_2 and other greenhouse gases is the burning of fossil fuels in power plants, and our automobiles, aircraft, trucks, trains, heating furnaces, etc. I also know that our contribution to the greenhouse effect has probably raised the average global temperature slightly over the last fifty years. Going forward, I know we must develop new energy sources that do not pollute and amplify the natural greenhouse effect. Until new technologies come along—and they will—I believe we should encourage and support both government and private research and development. Finally, I hope that people and the media will reject unscientific doom-and-gloom opinions and snake oil salesmen on the issue of global warming and climate change.

> My glass is half full on this subject, and I have faith that fifty or seventy-five years from now this problem may be resolved. In my opinion, developing safe fusion power (power of the sun) for electricity generation and mastering nonpolluting ways to overcome gravity are the keys to the future.

CHAPTER 10

Guns and the Military

Why should Americans revere the privilege of owning guns? Why combine guns and the military in one chapter? What should responsible people do when they purchase their first gun?

I have to say that the wisdom of the Founding Fathers never ceases to amaze me every time I reflect on American history. They knew that all governments inevitably drift toward tyranny (absolute power vested in a single leader), and, if unopposed, tyrannies eventually start slaughtering those citizens who oppose them. We have seen this happen many times in the last hundred years in countries such as Russia, China, Germany, Turkey, and Vietnam, to name but a few. The tendency toward bloody tyranny by governments against their own citizens has put millions of people to death in the twentieth century alone, a practice known as *genocide*.

The Founding Fathers had just won liberty for the Colonies from the British Empire through a bloody rebellion that began with a gun-control raid by the redcoats in Lexington and Concord on April 19, 1775. The purpose of the raid was to take away any weapons and "domesticate" the colonists. When the Revolutionary War finally ended, the founders designed a federal government based on the Constitution that included the Second Amendment to ensure that American citizens could always retain weapons capable of overthrowing the federal government *when* it became tyrannical. I stress the word *when*, not *if*, because the founders knew this would happen sometime in the future.

The Second Amendment is our insurance against genocide.

The Second Amendment to the US Constitution protects the *right* of the people to keep and bear arms and was adopted on December 15, 1791, as part of the first ten amendments contained in the Bill of Rights. The Second Amendment states, in full, "A well-regulated militia, being necessary to the security of a free state, the right of the people to keep and bear arms shall not be infringed." Serious challenges to the Second Amendment began in the 1960s and have continued unabated ever since. It was only in 2008, in *District of Columbia v. Heller,* that the Supreme Court ruled the Second Amendment applied to an individual's right to own a gun. However, efforts by the liberal Left continue to convince the American people that the Second Amendment to the Constitution is now obsolete. Gun crimes, especially mass shootings, are used to support the thought that Americans should give up their guns. Knowing that overturning the Second Amendment is practically impossible because it would take three-fourths of the states to concur, liberals continually chip away at gun rights at the federal, state, and local levels by making gun ownership more and more difficult through onerous gun laws.

> What is overlooked is the real problem with guns in our American culture: a combination of crime, mental illness, and poor parenting. Smart people have realized that guns don't kill people; people kill people.

I want to get back to the reason our founders wrote the Second Amendment. Arming citizens—or at least giving citizens the right to bear arms—is an effective way to convince potential tyrants that any effort to become a "Manchurian candidate" (a tyrant in hiding) in this country will eventually be put down by American citizens. American citizens already own hundreds of millions of guns and billions of rounds of ammunition. This is what the Constitution calls the militia, citizen patriot soldiers. The citizen militia is a formidable force against tyranny, if needed. It is perhaps the best internal security force we have because a tyrant would initially control military forces and law enforcement. If some type of Manchurian candidate did emerge, any ordered use of police, military or the National Guard against the population would quickly fail because the thought of Americans killing Americans is inconceivable—not just to me but probably to most other Americans, regardless of political beliefs. A well-armed civilian population is also a powerful force against any external force that might desire to take over our country.

A dose of recent history may add some meat to the argument against disarming the population. The twentieth century was a killing field in countries where the government implemented a gun confiscation policy and later decided to "tame and cleanse the population" (that is, engage in genocide). The following examples demonstrate how disarming the population allows a government to commit genocide at will:

- Turkey implemented gun control in 1911, and 1.5 million Christian Armenians were exterminated between 1915 and 1917.

- The Soviet Union established gun control in 1929, and about 20 million dissidents were rounded up and murdered between 1929 and 1953.
- Germany established gun control in 1938. By 1945, more than 10 million Jews, intellectuals, political dissidents, gypsies, mentally ill and physically disabled people had been exterminated across much of Europe.
- China established gun control in 1935. About 20 million political dissidents were rounded up and exterminated between 1948 and 1952.
- Cambodia established gun control in 1956. The government rounded up about 1 million educated people and exterminated them between 1975 and 1977.
- Guatemala established gun control in 1964. Subsequently, one hundred thousand Mayan Indians were rounded up and killed between 1981 and 1984.
- Uganda established gun control in 1970, and three hundred thousand Christians were rounded up and murdered from 1971 to 1979.

Although the emergence of a tyrannical government in the United States interested in confiscating civilian-owned guns seems remote, who knows what the future will bring?

Private gun ownership comes with special responsibilities. The most frequent reasons I hear for wanting a gun are self-defense, protection of family, hunting, and target shooting at a gun range with family and friends. Responsible ownership includes a course in gun safety, learning how to use the gun, learning how to clean and maintain it, and obtaining the required permit to carry it concealed if that's what you want. I have owned guns for sixty years and have a permit to carry. A few years ago, my wife said she would like a gun for self-defense, so I bought her a small nine-millimeter handgun. The first thing she did was attend gun school taught by a retired marine gunnery sergeant. She learned handgun safety and everything about her new gun: how to load it, how to shoot it in various positions, how to maintain it, and how to store it. This course required passing a final written exam and shooting test to obtain the certificate.

I was proud of her for becoming a responsible handgun owner. While she had previously shot handguns and rifles at family outings, she was basically afraid of them until taking this course.

Another responsibility of family gun ownership is keeping guns inaccessible to children unless under direct adult supervision. I believe that children should be educated on gun safety and be allowed to shoot only with direct adult supervision. Many kids have natural curiosity about guns, so the best way to prevent inappropriate use is to allow supervised shooting, while emphasizing and demonstrating gun safety. Storage of guns in homes with children needs some thought. A gun safe with thumbprint or retinal-scan access would be my choice if we still had kids.

The military is our primary defense against external threats. The best and most effective way to manage external threats is to have the best and most formidable armed force with the best and most lethal technology. Based on lessons painfully learned in World War II, the US has built the most formidable and capable military in the world. In my view, we need to keep it that way. Unfortunately, military readiness and advanced lethal technology has been cyclic. Republicans/Conservatives in general have been more willing to spend money on military readiness and capability than Democrats/Liberals. For example, insufficient military spending during the eight-year Obama administration seriously degraded our military capability, and military spending during the previous eight-year Bush administration was increased but wasted on the war in Iraq, which has proved to be a war we didn't need to fight.

For what it is worth, I think our military should stay out of foreign wars unless we are attacked. We should keep our military the best in the world and spend our wealth on infrastructure instead of foreign wars. I also believe that we should stop spending taxpayer dollars on defending Europe at the current levels. If Europe doesn't step forward and pay for most of their own defense, we should consider withdrawing from NATO and spending that money on US infrastructure.

God bless America! Keep our military the best on earth. Learn gun safety and how to shoot—shooting at your local club and range is fun for the whole family. Be willing to pass the ammunition around in case citizens need to mobilize to put down tyranny.

CHAPTER 11

Health Care

Who is responsible for health care for you and your family? Is health care an entitlement? Who should pay for your health care? Should people be able to select the type and extent of coverage they need? Who is best at providing affordable health care (federal government, state government, employers, individuals)?

A ll Americans have access to quality health care services; it's just a question of who pays for it! There is no doubt that medical capabilities and services in the US are among the best in the world. Why put private health insurers out of business just so the government can take over.

The founding documents of the United States do not establish a right to health care. The preamble to the US Constitution states, "promote the general welfare"; it does *not* state that health care will be provided by the federal government. The Constitution's Bill of Rights lists personal freedoms that the government cannot infringe upon; it does *not* contain a list of services that the federal government must provide. Nevertheless, the US medical system, one of the best in the world, has evolved through private enterprise without the federal government.

I believe it is the responsibility of individuals to provide health insurance for themselves and their families, just like they do with auto, home, or life insurance. In American culture, it is not the government's role to provide health insurance. The United States, Greece, and Poland are the only countries of the thirty-four members of the Organization of Economic Cooperation and Development (OECD) that do not have a mandated government-controlled health care system. So, what?! I am okay with other countries that prefer a socialist approach to medical services; that is one way to do it. However, socialized medicine is not consistent with our

Constitution and the American way. Socialism, by definition, means government control of the distribution of goods and services, and our health care system makes up about 20 percent of the whole economy. Under the single-payer system favored by the liberal Left in this country, everyone has a right to free health care and all health care bills would be paid by the government. *Free* is the operative word. Just wait until you see your new tax withholding in your paycheck and realize that you might have to sell the house and at least one of your cars because your take-home pay drops by 20 to 30 percent.

You may get the impression that I don't care about people who don't have health insurance, but that would be a mistake. According to the US Census Bureau, 33 million people in the United States (10.4 percent of the US population) did not have health insurance in 2014. Everyone in the US has access to the best health care available on the planet, but some decline to purchase health insurance. They may not want it because they are young and don't need it, they want it but can't afford it, they have a preexisting condition that prevents obtaining insurance at a reasonable cost, or they choose to pay for medical services out of pocket as needed. Among the reasons that worry me most are those who simply can't afford health insurance or can't get insurance at a reasonable cost because of preexisting conditions.

Solutions for improving health care affordability have been made, and will continue to be made, to the existing system without resorting to single-payer socialistic measures. Based on promises made by President Trump, I expect significant changes for the better in our health care system in the next year or so, when Congress makes health care a high priority again. Making changes to our existing health care system in a hyperpolitical election year is impossible, so we will just have to wait until Congress addresses it again.

CHAPTER 12

Final Thoughts

My goal in writing this book was to share a candid personal commentary on politics, social issues, and contemporary life. The book is intentionally short, so it can be read in one sitting. I suspect it may resonate with centrist and right-leaning readers, but I hope that some left-leaning readers may take something away from the read. Additionally, I intended to offer young people with some advice on developing character, values, and a reliable moral compass—as well as practical advice for succeeding in life.

I have no special insight, just 71 years of life experiences with education, marriage, raising kids, helping to raise four grandkids, family dynamics, making friends, worldwide travel for business and pleasure, a forty-year career in nuclear power plant safety, and a keen interest in history, politics, and social issues.

Sharing life's operating experience with those who have a limited amount is important to me. Young people don't have much life operating experience yet, and older people may not share their experiences unless asked. Sadly, there may not be a good way to exchange this type information between the young and old, and this gets to the core reason for writing this book. Younger people may find it easier to accept or consider this type of information from someone they don't know with some age-related credibility. I wish you all the best in your life journey, and I hope you will freely share your life operating experience with people you care about.

Since writing this book, my wife and I have sold our retirement home in Acworth, Georgia, bought an RV, and have left for an extended tour of North America over the next couple of years. We now will get to see those places we didn't see during past vacations and travels.

For those who read my book, I welcome your feedback. I am on Facebook.

www.ingramcontent.com/pod-product-compliance
Lightning Source LLC
Chambersburg PA
CBHW050417290526
45786CB00003B/1294